# KID START-UP

## HOW **YOU** CAN BE AN ENTREPRENEUR

## MARK CUBAN, SHAAN PATEL, & IAN McCUE

DIVERSION
BOOKS

Diversion Books
A Division of Diversion Publishing Corp.
443 Park Avenue South, Suite 1004
New York, NY 10016
www.diversionbooks.com

For more information, email info@diversionbooks.com

First Diversion Books edition August 2018.
Paperback ISBN: 978-1-63576-472-7
eBook ISBN: 978-1-63576-471-0

Printed in the U.S.A.
SDB/1808
    7 9 10 8 6

# ABOUT THE AUTHORS

## Mark Cuban

Since the age of 12, Mark has been a natural entrepreneur. Selling garbage bags door to door, the seed was planted early on for what would eventually become long-term success. Cuban is now an American billionaire businessman, investor, film producer, author, television personality, philanthropist, and serial entrepreneur. He is the owner of the NBA's Dallas Mavericks, Landmark Theaters, and Magnolia Pictures, and the chairman of AXS TV. He is also a "shark" investor on ABC's hit primetime television show *Shark Tank*. Cuban is also the author of the bestseller *How To Win At The Sport of Business*.

## Shaan Patel

Shaan has always been an entrepreneur at heart. In elementary school, he sold Pokemon cards. In middle school, he sold music CDs. In high school, he made thousands off internet referrals. In college, he made tens of thousands selling used iPhones on eBay. After achieving a perfect score on the SAT, Shaan founded his real business: Prep Expert—a test prep company offering SAT & ACT prep classes in twenty cities and online. Shaan appeared on *Shark Tank* to pitch Prep Expert and closed an investment deal with Mark Cuban. Patel is also the author of multiple bestselling SAT & ACT prep books.

## Ian McCue

Ian is the founder and director of Spark Skill, an educational startup offering coding, design, and maker summer camps for tweens and teens. At just 16 years old, he is an entrepreneur with extensive experience in STEM and educational ventures, along with a passion for promoting youth engagement in coding, engineering, and business development.

# LETTER FROM THE AUTHORS

Welcome! Every day, parents and their kids ask us for ideas on what kinds of businesses kids can start and run. Believe it or not, there are plenty of businesses that kids as young as 8 or 9 years old can start doing! Running a lemonade stand for a few hours is a great experience. However, there are so many more ways for a kid to not only gain valuable experience in the business world, but to earn some extra money as well.

We hope our book, *Kid Start-Up*, will give kids a great head start to launching their own age-appropriate business.

Let us know your thoughts by emailing us at:
feedback@kidstartupbook.com

**Mark, Shaan, and Ian**

# TABLE OF CONTENTS

CHAPTER **1**

# WHAT IS AN
# ENTREPRENEUR?

# WHAT DO YOU WANT TO BE WHEN YOU GROW UP?

Have you ever been asked: "What do you want to be when you grow up?" Most kids reply with the following:

"I want to be a doctor."

"I want to be a lawyer."

"I want to be an engineer."

But have you ever heard someone say, "I want to be an entrepreneur"? Probably not. That's because most people don't know what an entrepreneur is.

The dictionary defines an entrepreneur as "a person who starts a business and is willing to risk loss in order to make money." Notice the key phrases in that definition: starts a business and to make money.

That's because this book is really about entrepreneurship. Any kid that starts a business to make money is an entrepreneur.

So the next time you get asked what you want to be when you grow up, you can respond, "I want to be an entrepreneur!"

"Entrepreneur" comes from the French word "entreprendre," which means "to undertake." And that's exactly what it means to be an entrepreneur. In order to be an entrepreneur, you just have "to undertake" a business. This is not the same thing as having an idea. Billions of people have ideas. But only a few people are willing to pursue those ideas and turn them into a real business.

Another word for anyone that starts a business is "founder." If you start a business called "Sweeties Lemonade Stand," then you are the founder of the Sweeties Lemonade Stand. So when you start a business, you can call yourself both an entrepreneur **and** a founder.

# SUCCESSES & FAILURES: IT'S ALL PART OF THE ENTREPRENEURSHIP GAME

It's not easy being an entrepreneur. You have to take a lot of risks. You risk your time. You risk your money. But you also have to risk what is often most special to people — your reputation. What if you fail? Most kids do not want to fail, which prevents them from starting a business.

Do not worry. Every entrepreneur shares this fear of failing. Just go for it. No one knows whether or not they will succeed. You need to figure things out as you go – that's the fun part about entrepreneurship!

Rejection is the necessary evil of entrepreneurship. There has never been an entrepreneur who succeeded without failing first. Steve Jobs, the founder of Apple, is no exception. In his 2005 graduation speech to Stanford University, Jobs described being fired from Apple in 1985 and says that it was the "best thing that ever happened to [him]."

Unlike many people who would quit after such a big rejection, Steve Jobs did not. He continued following his love of technology by starting two other very successful companies. It is this kind of passion that makes entrepreneurs like Steve Jobs great. Jobs would later go back to Apple when the company saw how successful he could be without them.

# KID ENTREPRENEURS START EARLY

The great thing about being a kid entrepreneur is that you are young. Being young is a huge advantage when it comes to being an entrepreneur. Entrepreneurs will often make many mistakes and fail multiple times before they succeed. So it's better to learn from your mistakes and failures when you are young, rather than when you are old. If you start businesses now as a kid, you will surely be a successful entrepreneur when you are older. This is because you have learned a lot about entrepreneurship as a kid, so you won't make the same mistakes again when you are an adult.

You have to start somewhere as an entrepreneur. The first business you start will probably not be a million-dollar business. But that's okay! If you keep starting businesses, working hard, and learning as you go, a future business that you start could certainly become a million-dollar business. But you have to start simple.

Entrepreneurs start early. You either are an entrepreneur or you're not. Although you may not know that you are an entrepreneur, you can set yourself on the path to becoming a great one if you start a business as a kid. The common thread among almost all entrepreneurs is that they were interested in starting a business from a very young age.

While the authors of this book are now all successful entrepreneurs and our companies have made millions of dollars, we all started out as kid entrepreneurs first. Mark Cuban started out by selling garbage bags door-to-door to neighbors as his first business. Shaan Patel started out by selling Pokemon cards to his friends in elementary school as his first business. Ian McCue started out by selling websites as his first business.

By starting a simple business as a kid, you will learn more about entrepreneurship than any class could ever teach you. You will learn about sales, costs, hard work, and more. But you have to get started by launching a simple business, even if it's as simple as opening a lemonade stand. If we can do it, you can do it.

# THE CHARACTERISTICS OF A SUCCESSFUL KID ENTREPRENEUR

Here are some key characteristics that all entrepreneurs have in common. Make sure that you start to develop these personality traits as a kid. The better you become at having these things now, the more successful you will likely be in your career as an entrepreneur.

### 1. Hard Working

All successful entrepreneurs are hard working. Starting a business and making money is not easy. If it was easy, everyone would do it. But only the few people that are willing to work harder than everyone else will actually succeed at entrepreneurship. We're going to teach you a lot of the basics of entrepreneurship in this book, but you have to be the one that works hard in order to make your first business a reality.

### 2. Enthusiastic

All successful entrepreneurs are enthusiastic. In order to work hard, you better be enthusiastic about your business. It is hard to work hard on something you don't love. Have you ever had a homework assignment that you hated doing? It's probably because you weren't enthusiastic about the subject. When you start a business, make sure that you love what you're doing. It will make it much easier to spend hours working on your business if you are enthusiastic about it.

### 3. Creative

All successful entrepreneurs are creative. Do you have a creative mind? If so, then you may be perfect for entrepreneurship. One of the most fun parts of being an entrepreneur is that you get to make all of the decisions. You get to be creative about what you're going to sell, where you're going to sell, and how you're going to sell it. You don't have to listen to anyone. You make the rules in entrepreneurship. Creative kids will love this aspect about starting a business.

### 4. Flexible

All successful entrepreneurs are flexible. A stubborn entrepreneur who is unwilling to change will likely fail. Often times during your journey in launching a business, you may run into roadblocks. For some reason you're not getting the sales that you expected or the business isn't working like you wanted. When this happens, good entrepreneurs don't quit. Instead, they become flexible. They try something different than the original plan to see if that works instead. Be flexible to succeed in launching your business.

### 5. Motivated

All successful entrepreneurs are motivated. You have to know why you want to start a business. Making money is certainly one goal of starting a business. But it shouldn't be the only goal. You have to be motivated by a bigger goal. An entrepreneur who is only motivated to make money will likely fail. Instead, figure out what motivates you to build your business. Once you figure out your goals, work hard to achieve those goals. Stay motivated to succeed in launching your business.

# THE GOAL OF ENTREPRENEURSHIP

So what is entrepreneurship all about? While most kids think that business is about making money, money is only one aspect of it. The end goal of any business is to create value for people.

You can create value by doing something useful, important, or good for other people. The goal of business should be to help other people by making their lives just a little bit better.

Here are some ways that you can add value as a kid entrepreneur:

1. You can **help** people with more options for gifts.

2. You can **help** people with storing money.

3. You can **help** people with saving time.

4. You can **help** people with health.

5. You can **help** people with food.

6. You can **help** people with cars.

7. You can **help** people with pets.

8. You can **help** people with sports.

9. You can **help** people with technology.

10. You can **help** people with shoveling snow.

As a matter of fact, in Chapter 5, we will give you 10 business ideas that will help people with all of the above that you can start immediately! Here are the businesses that you will learn how to start:

1. A **business** that sells scented soaps.

2. A **business** that sells duct tape wallets.

3. A **business** that sells garbage bags.

4. A **business** that sells water bottles.

5. A **business** that sells lemonade.

6. A **business** that washes cars.

7. A **business** that walks dogs.

8. A **business** that makes shoelaces.

9. A **business** that helps seniors with technology.

10. A **business** that shovels snow.

Notice how in the first list, the keyword was **"help."** In the second list, the keyword was **"business."** That's because you can't have one without the other. A successful business must help people in some way. **If you're looking to both make money and help people, then entrepreneurship is for you.**

# HELP PEOPLE + MAKE MONEY
# = BUSINESS

Entrepreneurship is about building something great that you love. There is nothing more fun and fulfilling. If you care about your idea and are willing to work hard, become an entrepreneur by starting a business.

# WHAT SUCCESSFUL ENTREPRENEURS SAY

Finally, let's end this chapter with some quotes by some famous entrepreneurs that you might know, including the stars of *Shark Tank*. Hopefully these quotes will motivate you as you begin your journey to start a business and make money.

> It comes down to finding something you love to do and then just trying to be great at it.
>
> —Mark Cuban, Star of ABC's *Shark Tank*

> As an entrepreneur, you love your business like a child, and you're taught to be laser-focused on the business.
>
> —Daymond John, Star of ABC's *Shark Tank*

> I'd rather invest in an entrepreneur who has failed, than one who assumes success from day one.
>
> —Kevin O'Leary, Star of ABC's *Shark Tank*

> Business is a sprint until you find an opportunity, then it's the patience of a marathon runner.
>
> —Robert Herjavec, Star of ABC's *Shark Tank*

> "My best successes came on the heels of failures.
>
> —Barbara Corcoran, Star of ABC's *Shark Tank*

> "I learned that nobody's better than you to get your business off the ground. The experience you get is priceless.
>
> —Lori Grenier, Star of ABC's *Shark Tank*

> "Whatever you do, do it well. Do it so well that when people see you do it, they will want to come back and see you do it again. And they will want to bring others and show them how well you do what you do.
>
> —Walt Disney, Founder of Disney

> "I'm convinced that about half of what separates successful entrepreneurs from the non-successful ones is pure perseverance.
>
> —Steve Jobs, Founder of Apple

> "Some people dream of success...while others wake up and work hard at it.
>
> —Mark Zuckerberg, Founder of Facebook

> "Obviously everyone wants to be successful, but I want to be looked back on as being very innovative, very trusted and ethical, and ultimately making a big difference in the world.
>
> —Larry Page, Co-Founder of Google

# SUMMARY

An entrepreneur is a person who starts a business to help people and make money. You can also call this person a "business owner" or "founder." Business is about building something great that you love. Classes can only teach you so much about starting a business. Entrepreneurship is best learned through the hands-on experience of starting a business yourself. Our next chapter covers how you can discover a business idea that is right for you, helps people, and makes money.

## Key Takeaways

* Entrepreneurs are people who start businesses to help people and make money.

* By starting a simple business as a kid, you will learn about sales, costs, hard work, and more.

* The skills you learn starting a simple business as a kid will help you start bigger businesses as you get older.

## Next Steps

Once you start selling products or services with the goals of helping people and making money, you are an entrepreneur. The best way to learn about entrepreneurship is to start your own business. Continue reading to discover your perfect business idea—something that you can launch TODAY!

# CHAPTER 2

## THE KID
## ENTREPRENEUR

# THE TIME ADVANTAGE

Not many kids are entrepreneurs. By starting a business and making money now, you will be part of a small group of kids that will go on to become successful adult entrepreneurs. The biggest advantage you have on your side is time. You have lots of time to make mistakes and learn from them.

Imagine an adult who is launching their first business at 50 years old. They don't have a lot of time to make mistakes and learn from them compared to the amount of time you have. By the time you are 50 years old, chances are that you will have started multiple different companies, some successful and some not-so-successful. The successful ones will be the ones that you are proud of and the not-so-successful ones will be the ones that teach you the most about entrepreneurship and business. Let's start learning now!

# THE STUDENT ENTREPRENEUR

As a kid entrepreneur, you are by definition a student entrepreneur. You should not quit school in order to start a business. School can give you a solid foundation to help you become a great entrepreneur. For example, school teaches you how to write. This is a very important skill to have as an entrepreneur since you will likely write marketing material, website content, pitches, and proposals as a future business owner.

Being a student entrepreneur is tough. Many adult entrepreneurs are not in school, so they can focus all of their time on their business. But you must focus on both school and your business. So that means you have to learn about time management in order to use your time efficiently. You will also have to make some sacrifices. For example, many of your friends may play video games for many hours on the weekend. Instead, you may want to spend your weekend time building your business. While your friends are enjoying their time now, you will enjoy your time later when you have a successful business. You put in hard work now in order to earn great rewards that you can enjoy later.

There is one big benefit to being a student entrepreneur though: you are forced to get more done in less time. Since you don't have as much time as someone who is not in school, you have to use your time more carefully. This will make you get more done in less time. For example, if you need to launch your business in a short 3-month summer that you have, then you will get it done. However, another entrepreneur who is not in school may not have a 3-month deadline in which he needs to launch his business. So it may take him years before he starts his business. But you did it in 3 months! All because you are a student entrepreneur that is forced to get more done in the less time that you have available to you.

# PRODUCTIVITY TIPS

Because you do not have as much time as someone who is not in school, here are some tips on how you can be more productive with the limited amount of time that you do have.

### 1. Do the Most Difficult Task First

You only have so much energy to spend in one day. And your ability to focus will go down as the day goes on. So you should complete the task that requires the most thinking first. If you complete your most difficult task early in the day, you will not feel as drained later on in the day when you have less difficult tasks to complete.

### 2. Turn Off the Tech

In order to really get work done, you should disconnect from technology that may distract you from building your business. In the world of Facebook, Instagram, Twitter, YouTube, and Snapchat, distractions are all around us. Because information is so readily available to us at all times of the day, it is hard for many of us to find time to focus without interruption. This is why we recommend turning off the tech when you want to get some serious work done.

### 3. Reply to E-mail Last

One of the biggest tasks that bogs down the entrepreneur's workday is e-mail. The world worked just fine when people weren't sending e-mails back and forth every few minutes. So it's not necessary to reply to every e-mail immediately. Most e-mails can wait. Set aside some time at the end of the day to reply to all of your e-mails at once. This way, sending e-mails doesn't stop your work. In addition, replying to e-mails is a rather easy task that typically doesn't spend a lot of mental energy. So it doesn't make sense to spend the beginning of your day replying to e-mails.

### 4. Set Daily Milestones

Starting a business is a big task, especially for a first-time entrepreneur. Where do you start? The answer is start anywhere. Just start with a small task that you think can finish. Then, do another task. Then another, and another. Eventually, you'll realize that starting a business was not as hard as it first appeared!

A large task becomes much easier if you chip away at it everyday. If you do not have a daily task that helps you get one step closer to launching your business, your progress will become slow because of the all-too-common of excuse of "I got busy with school."

### 5. Take One Weekend Night Off

You might think that this tip means to take one weekend night off in order to relax. But it's actually the opposite. You should spend Friday or Saturday of every weekend to focus on working on your business. Use the other night to watch TV, play games, spend time with family and friends, or do whatever else you enjoy.

The reality of a student entrepreneur is that your weekends and nights are no longer for relaxing, but for your working on your business. If you are truly enthusiastic about your business, you won't mind. When you are launching your business, you should care about it more than anything else.

# 66 Six Quotes the Most Successful Kid Entrepreneurs Say Every Day 99

Succeeding at business doesn't happen by coincidence. Here are six quotes the most successful kid entrepreneurs say everyday in order to create their own future!

### 1. "One Day at a Time."

School can get busy. Instead of becoming overwhelmed with classes, exams, sports, and extracurricular activities, successful entrepreneurs take each day as it comes by completing as much as they possibly can for both school and their business in one 24-hour period.

### 2. "One Task at a Time."

Multitasking does not work. Trying to work your business while on Facebook chat is a bad idea. Successful entrepreneurs focus on one task at a time.

### 3. "I Will Make Money."

Business success is a mindset. Successful entrepreneurs not only believe they will make money, but they will work nonstop in order to get it.

### 4. "Two Hours for Business."

Time management is a key life skill. Blocking out time for working on your business is essential to building a successful business. Successful entrepreneurs will make sure that their business time is uninterrupted because they make it a priority.

### 5. "My Reward Will Be..."

Working too hard can be unhealthy. Sometimes you

need to relax. Successful entrepreneurs block out time to watch TV, hang out with friends, and do other fun activities.

### 6. "My Goal Is to..."

You cannot work hard if you don't have a goal. While it's great that your parents want you to succeed in business, this external motivation is not enough. You need to have internal motivation of wanting to do well yourself. Successful entrepreneurs not only know exactly how much money they want to make, but they also write down their goals.

## POP QUIZ: What is the best predictor of success for entrepreneurs?

A: Smarts

B: Emotional Smarts

C: Self-Control

D: Creativity

The answer: **self-control**. Self-control is the most universal and accurate predictor of success. If you want to be successful, you need to be able to manage emotions and work hard. All of this requires significant self-control.

However, having self-control is harder than ever today. Technology has added numerous distractions to our daily lives: e-mail, text messaging, Facebook, Instagram, Snapchat, Twitter, YouTube, Netflix, etc. Having the self-control to avoid all of these enticing platforms is no easy task.

This quiz was inspired by social psychologist Dr. Victoria Brescoll at Yale University. Professor Brescoll pointed to the famous Stanford marshmallow experiment as proof that self-control is crucial to success.

In the 1972 experiment, researchers would place a 4-6 year-old child in a room with just a marshmallow. The children were told that they could eat the one marshmallow now, but if they waited 15 minutes, they would be rewarded with two marshmallows. This experiment was conducted on over 600 children. **Only a third of the children were able to exercise enough self-control to not eat the marshmallow immediately.** Years later, these children were found to be more successful based on many life outcomes:

* Earning more money

* Being more popular with friends, classmates, and teachers

* Having better health

* Scoring 210 points higher on average on the SAT exam

Many other studies have continuously found that self-control is a massive predictor of achievement. What's the secret to business success as a kid entrepreneur? Self-control.

## Fun Video Time

If you want to laugh, watch the reactions of the children in this remake of the Stanford marshmallow experiment:

**www.kidstartupbook.com/marshmallow**

# SUMMARY

-------------------------------------------------------------

While it is not easy being a student entrepreneur, there is a huge benefit: you accomplish more in less time! In order to make the most of your spare time, remember to complete the most difficult tasks first; turn off the tech; reply to e-mail last; set daily milestones; and take one weekend night off. Work on improving your self-control in order to succeed as a kid entrepreneur.

## Key Takeaways

* Kid entrepreneurs accomplish more in less time.

* A strategic approach to your spare time will help you to successfully manage your business, even with a busy schedule.

* Self-control is the key to success in business — and much of life.

## Next Steps

Review these productivity tips and start practicing them in your daily life. They force you to develop self-control, enabling you to achieve more in less time. Schedule time to work on your business, and truly focus to make the most of it!

CHAPTER **3**

## DISCOVERING
## YOUR BUSINESS IDEA

# IMPROVE LIFE ONE CUP OF LEMONADE AT A TIME

You now know what entrepreneurship is, and how an entrepreneur can succeed. Let's start identifying some business ideas! Every successful business is built on a simple idea that makes life better. This improvement can be tiny, yet still change the world!

What could you do to make life a little bit better?

Our business ideas in this book include washing cars, selling home goods, and making unique shoelaces. So, how do these improve life?

* Washing cars: keeps cars looking fresh

* Selling home goods: reduces time spent shopping and saves customers' money

* Seling unique shoelaces: adds a pop of fun to any pair of shoes

How would the next three ideas improve life?

SELLING WATER BOTTLES

WALKING DOGS

MAKING SCENTED SOAPS

Even simple ideas can make life better. So, how do you come up with your own ideas, and how do you choose one? Let's dive in.

# DISCOVERING YOUR OWN IDEAS

What products or services could improve your life? Think through your day from start to finish. Did you do any chores that you could have paid someone else to do? What could have been improved?

When you try to come up with a list of business ideas, follow these two steps:

1. Find a problem, no matter how small, in your daily life.

2. Come up with a product or service that could solve this problem.

Here are the steps for three of our business ideas:

## Washing cars

1. My parents have to go to the car wash often. It costs $10, and it takes so long.

2. I could take the $10 that they pay, wash their cars myself, and save them time and effort.

## Selling home goods

1. Buying trash bags and other essentials at grocery stores in small numbers is convenient, but expensive.

2. I could buy large numbers of these products at cheaper stores, and then sell them for more in my neighborhood. My customers would save money, and I would make money.

## Selling unique shoelaces

1. My old shoes could use a pop of color. I'd love to support my school's sports team, too.

2. I could buy shoe laces that match my school colors. My shoes would look as good as new!

# Write the steps that you could have taken to discover these ideas:

**Walking dogs:**

1. ---------------------------------------------------

---------------------------------------------------

2. ---------------------------------------------------

---------------------------------------------------

**Selling water bottles:**

1. ---------------------------------------------------

---------------------------------------------------

2. ---------------------------------------------------

---------------------------------------------------

**Making scented soaps:**

1. ---------------------------------------------------

---------------------------------------------------

2. ---------------------------------------------------

---------------------------------------------------

# Now, come up with three of your own ideas by following the steps:

**Idea #1:**

1. _____

_____

2. _____

_____

**Idea #2:**

1. _____

_____

2. _____

_____

**Idea #3:**

1. _____

_____

2. _____

_____

# SELECTING THE WINNER

Not all ideas will make a good business. Some can become million-dollar companies, and others can't. Some are expensive to start, and others can be started for free. So, how do you pick an idea?

You may be surprised that you should not pick the idea that could make you the most money, or the idea that would cost you the least. Instead, you should pick the idea that **you will be best at**, and that you will **work the hardest at**. If you aren't talented or skilled at something, it is not a good idea to start a business doing it. If you aren't willing to work hard on a business idea, it isn't for you.

Other than that, it's up to you! If you have many ideas that you are good at and will work hard at, talk to your friends and family to hear their opinions. Maybe they see you as even more talented at something than you think you are!

# SUMMARY

---------------------------------------------------

Successful businesses are built on simple ideas that make life better – even just a little bit better. Ask yourself: "What can I do to make life a little bit better?" Find a problem that you face in your daily life and come up with a product or service that could solve this problem. Think about your talents and skills, and don't hesitate to ask your family and friends what you're good at. Choose the business idea that you will be best at, and that you will work the hardest at.

## Key Takeaways

* Entrepreneurs create businesses to solve problems that people face, no matter how small the problems may seem.

* Discovering a good business idea requires that you solve a problem that people face in their daily lives.

* Entrepreneurs succeed when they work hard and use their talents.

## Next Steps

Think about problems in your life that you would not only be great at solving, but that you would also work hard at solving. These are your winning business ideas!

# CHAPTER 4

# 10 BUSINESSES ANY KID CAN START

**1**

# SCENTED SOAPS

## Materials & Costs

| | |
|---|---|
| Microwave Safe Bowl | – |
| Spatula or Mixing Utensil | – |
| 20 Small Bars with Recommended Kit: Everything Lavender Soap Making Kit By ArtMinds™ (Included in Kit: Base, Color. Flowers, Fragrance) | $1 / Soap Bar |
| Additional Items: Bags with Ties | $0.05 / Soap Bar |

**Total Cost: $1.05** per Soap Bar

## Sale Price

**SALES STRATEGY**

**$3**
One

**$5**
Two

Revenue:
**$3 to $5** per Sale

### Bundle Goods

**Reduce your price per item** when people buy more of them. In this business, you will profit $2 if you sell one bar, or $3 if you sell two bars.

People will be more likely to purchase two bars because of the lower price per bar of soap.

**One bar:** $3 - $1.05 = **$1.95** of Profit

**Two bars:** $5 - $2.10 = **$2.90** of Profit

## MAKE IT! A Visual How-To Guide

**A.** Place half of the soap in a microwave-safe bowl and, with a parent's assistance, microwave it in 30 second intervals until melted.

**B.** Add one drop of color, two drops of fragrance, and a large sprinkle of Lavender Flowers and mix.

**C.** Pour the complete mix carefully into your molds, filling them halfway. Wait an hour, then remove and individually wrap in clear bags.

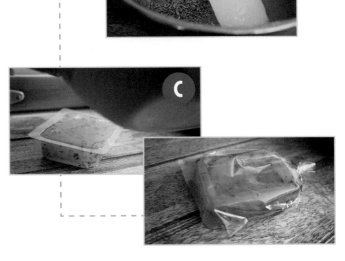

## SELL IT!

**Etsy. Sell your soaps** on the largest online handmade goods store! Visit **Etsy.com** to learn how.

**Farmer's Market. Set up shop in a local farmer's market** to have your customers come to you! Find a regular, local market near you, bring some samples, and spend a day talking to their customers and sellers about your business. They will likely have excellent advice for your product, sales, and local laws that could apply.

# DUCT TAPE WALLETS

## Lightweight Wallets

Recommended Age Range: 7 - 9 Years Old
Parental Supervision Recommended

Almost everyone has a wallet, but most wallets are far too bulky and bland. These easy-to-make duct tape wallets are easy to customize, and will make a great profit for you.

## Materials & Cost

Ruler & Scissor                                           –

Duct Tape: $0.50 / wallet                     $0.50 / wallet

**Total Cost: $0.50** per wallet

## Price Range

**$5**        **$8**        **$10**

Low        Ideal        High

Revenue: **$8** per Sale

$8 - $0.50 = **$7.50** of Profit per wallet

## MAKE IT! A Visual How-To Guide

**A.** Prepare your materials. We will refer to our black duct tape as the main tape, and our silver duct tape as the style tape. Feel free to use whatever colors of tape you would like on each step!

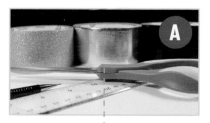

**B.** Cut four pieces of your tape to be eight inches long each.

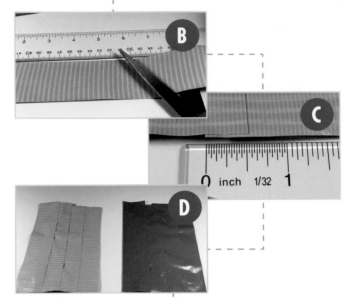

**C.** Overlap each piece of tape by half of an inch.

**D.** Repeat steps B and C using the style tape.

**E.** Stack the two rectangles on top of each other, sticky sides together. Start from one side and work your way to the other to reduce air bubbles.

**F.** Cut a ten-inch piece of style tape in in half lengthwise so that it is long and thin. Take one half and fold it over the top of the rectangle. Take the other half and fold it over the bottom. Trim the edges.

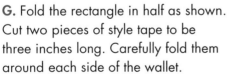

**G.** Fold the rectangle in half as shown. Cut two pieces of style tape to be three inches long. Carefully fold them around each side of the wallet.

**H.** Trim the excess tape.

**I.** Cut two pieces of primary tape to be slightly longer than the wallet. Carefully and fully overlap these pieces to make a pocket.

**J.** Cut two pieces of style tape two inches long. Carefully align them to either side of the newly added pocket, and fold them over, attaching the pocket's sides to the wallet.

**K.** Cut another piece of style tape to be slightly longer than the wallet. Rest the bottom of the wallet on the middle of the tape. Fold the tape over, sealing the bottom. Remove excess from the sides.

**L.** Trim a piece of style tape to be slightly taller than the wallet. Cut it in half lengthwise, making it long and thin. Carefully align it with the middle of the pocket, place it, and then fold the excess into the interior of the wallet.

**M.** Make more! Try mixing up the colors of duct tape.

# SELL IT!

**Door to Door.** Go from one house to the next with your parent and a few of your wallets. Knock on the door, and start with something like this: "Hi, I'm _____! Would you be interested in a lightweight Duct Tape Wallet?"

**Social Media.** Ask your friends and family to share your wallets on Facebook and Instagram. Send them a picture of the wallet with your phone number or email address in the background as seen above.

# 3  HOME GOODS

## Materials & Costs

Trash Bags                                              $0.10 / bag

**Total Cost: $0.10 per bag**

## Sale Price

**$2**                    **$3**                    Revenue: **$2 - 3** per Sale

Ten                    Twenty
Bags                   Bags

**Ten Bags:** $2 - (10 x $0.10) = **$1.00** of Profit

**Twenty Bags:** $3 - (20 x $0.10) = **$1.00** of Profit

## SELL IT!

**Door to Door.** Go from one house to the next with your parent and a couple of large boxes of trash bags. Knock on the door, and start with something like this: "Hi, does your family use garbage bags?" If they start to object, say, "Of course you use garbage bags, and I bet you pay more than fifteen cents a piece." (This sales strategy is from Mark Cuban's First Entrepreneurial Venture.)

## 4 WATER BOTTLES

## Materials & Costs

| | |
|---|---|
| Large Cooler | – |
| Ice for Cooler: $0.05 / Bottle | $0.05 / Bottle |
| Water Bottles: $0.20 / Bottle | $0.20 / Bottle |

**Total Cost: $0.25 per Bottle**

## Sale Price

**$1** 1 Bottle

**Revenue: $1 per Sale**

$1 - $0.25 = **$0.75** of Profit

## SELL IT!

**High Traffic Events.** Set up a small stand at a local youth event sports game (with permission from the location). The number of potential customers is a great boost to business!

**BONUS POINTS**

Choose a hot day outdoors in a place with lots of foot traffic for killer sales!

**Walking Trails and Parks.** Walk around your local trails or parks and offer your cold water bottles to people for just $1. Although these locations have fewer people, it is often easier to get permission to set up shop.

# 5 LEMONADE

Recommended Age Range: 10 - 12 Years Old
Parental Supervision Recommended

## Materials & Costs

| | | |
|---|---|---|
| Large Pitcher | – |
| Mixing Tool | – |
| Mug or Coffee Cup | – |
| Hot Filtered Water | – |
| Standard Measuring Cups | – |
| Half a Cup of Sugar | $1.00 / Pitcher |
| Half a Cup of Lemon Juice | $1.50 / Pitcher |
| Two and a Half Cups of Filtered Water | $0.05 / Pitcher |
| Two and a Half Cups of Ice | $0.05 / Pitcher |
| Plastic Cups and Straws | $0.05 / Cup |
| Mint Leaves | $0.05 / Cup |

Cost per Pitcher: **$2.60** • Cups per Pitcher: **8** • Cost per Cup: **$0.43**

## Sale Price

**$1**  1 Cup - Ideal

Revenue: **$1** per Sale

$1 - $0.43 = **$0.57** of Profit per Cup

## MAKE IT! A Visual How-to Guide

**A.** Pour around half a cup of hot water into a mug or coffee cup, and immediately add half a cup of sugar. Mix to dissolve for three minutes.

**B.** Pour half a cup of lemon juice, two and a half cups of filtered water, and the dissolved sugar into the pitcher. Mix briefly, then add two and a half cups of ice. Add a large branch of mint leaves for decoration.

**C.** When someone purchases a cup, fill it, leaving an inch of space at the top. Add a mint leaf.

## SELL IT!

**High Traffic Events.** Set up a small stand at a local youth event sports game (with permission from the location). The volume of potential customers is a great boost to business!

**Social Media.** Create a Facebook event for your lemonade stand. Have your friends and family share it and invite people to join!

# 6 CAR WASH CRAZE

Recommended Age Range: 10 - 12 Years Old
Parental Supervision Recommended

## Materials & Costs

| | |
|---|---|
| Sponges | – |
| Rags/Towels | – |
| Two Buckets of Water | – |
| Car Wash Soap: $1.00 / Car | $1.00 / Car |

**Cost per Car: $1.00**

## Service Price

**$9** Exterior Hand Wash   Revenue: **$9** per Wash

$9 - $1 = **$8** of Profit per Wash

## WASH IT! A Visual How-to Guide

**A.** Add car wash soap as directed to one of the buckets of water. Place a sponge in each bucket of water.

**B.** Rinse the outside of the car with the sponge from the bucket of clean, plain water.

**C.** Use the sponge from the bucket of soapy water to scrub the car.

**D.** Repeat step B.

**E.** Use clean rags/ towels to gently dry the outside of the car.

## SELL IT!

**Door to Door.** Go from one house to the next with flyers for your service. Ring the doorbell. If they answer, briefly introduce yourself, saying, "Hi, I'm ____, the neighborhood car washer! Here is my contact information (hand them a flyer), and note that the first wash is free! Please let me know if I can ever be of assistance!"

**SALES STRATEGY**

**Free Trial**

Offer a free car wash to potential repeat customers! If you do a great job, they are very likely to continue using your service on a regular basis. Reserve this offer for neighbors and friends.

**Local Events.** Set up a small stand at a gym or park (with permission from the location). People will be busy at the event, and it is an ideal time for them to get a car wash.

# 7 NEIGHBORHOOD DOG WALKING

## Materials & Costs

 Two Dog Leashes —

## Service Price

**$10** — **$15**

Half Hour    Full Hour

Revenue:
**$10 to $15** per Walk

### Reducing Risk

**In order to provide a quality service** and reduce your risk, only walk as many dogs as you can realistically control. We recommend handling no more than two at a time. However, charge the same prices regardless of whether your customer has one or two dogs.

**Half Hour:** $10 of Profit per Walk

**Full Hour:** $15 of Profit per Walk

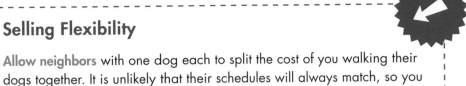

### Selling Flexibility

Allow neighbors with one dog each to split the cost of you walking their dogs together. It is unlikely that their schedules will always match, so you will often still collect the full price from each happy customer. Make sure that their dogs are friendly to each other first.

## SELL IT!

**Door to Door.** Go from one house to the next with flyers for your service. Ring the doorbell. If they answer, briefly introduce yourself, saying, "Hi, I'm ____, the neighborhood dog walker! Here is my contact information (hand them a flyer), and note that the first half hour walk is free! Please let me know if I can ever help!"

**Social Media.** List your job on Facebook as "Neighborhood Dog Walker." With owners' permission, post photos of you walking dogs every so often. This will help ensure that you stay fresh in the minds of potential customers.

### Free Trial

Offer a free, half-hour walk to each potential customer! Once they see how happy their dog is, they are more likely to continue using your services.

SALES STRATEGY

# 8 UNIQUE SHOELACES

## Materials & Costs

Cotton Shoelaces                                        $3.00 / Pair

Cost per Shoelace: **$3.00**

## Sale Price

**$10**
Low

**$14**
Ideal

**$19**
High

Revenue: **$14** per Sale

$14 - $3 = **$11** of Profit per Shoelaces

## SELL IT!

**Etsy.** Sell your shoelaces on the largest online handmade goods store! Visit **Etsy.com** today to learn how.

**High Traffic Events.** Set up a small stand at a local youth event sports game (with permission from the location). Sell lots of shoelaces that match the competing teams' colors. The volume of likely customers is a great boost to business!

### Referral Marketing

Let your friends and peers work for you! Every time that someone you know finds a shoelace buyer for you, give them $3 of your profit on that sale. They will be motivated to help you as much as possible!

**SALES STRATEGY**

# 9 SENIOR TECH HELP

Smartphone, Tablet,
Computer, and Social
Media Training and Troubleshooting

Recommended Age Range: 10 - 12 Years Old
Parental Supervision Recommended

## Service Price

**$20** — **$30**

Half Hour    Full Hour

Revenue:
**$20 to $30**

### Capitalize on Your Skills

In order to provide a quality service ask your client what they need before scheduling a time with them. This will allow you to better judge how long you will need, and to ensure that you know how to fix the issues that they need help with.

## SELL IT!

**Customers List.** Talk to your friends and family and come up with a list of people who may be interested in your services. Determine what about your service will be valuable to them, write down what you will say, and then contact them (typically through email or phone). Note their response and what you learned from it.

**Social Media.** List your job on Facebook as "Senior Tech Help." Post photos with your clients (and their approval) every so often. This will help make sure that you stay fresh in the minds of potential customers.

# 10 SNOW SHOVELING

## Materials & Costs

 Snow Shovel                                    _

## Service Price

**$20**
First
Half Hour

**$10**
Every
Additional
Half Hour

Revenue:
**$20+**

### Snow Shoveling Tips

* Keep your knees bent

* Keep your back straight

* Lift with your legs, not with your back *Do not try to lift a lot at once

* Start by clearing only what is necessary for the car to pull out of the driveway

## SELL IT!

**Door to Door.** Go from house to house in your neighborhood with flyers for your service. Ring the doorbell. If they answer, briefly introduce yourself, saying, "Hi, I'm ____, and I shovel snow in the neighborhood! Here is my contact information (hand them a flyer), and note that your first half hour is free! Please call me if I can ever be of assistance!"

**SALES STRATEGY**

### Seasonal Snow Strategy

Snow creates a storm of demand for this business during the winter season. Talk to your neighbors as winter approaches, and don't give up on selling your service until the season is over!

# SUMMARY

Business ideas do not need to be complicated. The best products and services for kids to sell are simple. Try to be creative when you sell your goods. Bundle them together and offer them at a lower price; visit farmer's markets and set up shop; and ask your friends and family to share your company on social media.

## Key Takeaways

* Your first business does not need to sell anything new or complicated! Keep it simple. It is easy to sell a product such as a water bottle because people already understand the value of the product in their lives.

* Make sure that your costs are not greater than your revenue. This will result in a negative profit, and your business will actually be losing money.

* Many adult businesses often take many months or even years before they are making money. But for your first simple business as a kid, focus on making money within the first few months of opening up shop.

## Next Steps

Choose a simple product or service – it will be a lot easier to sell! Think creatively about how you will sell your product, and read on to learn how other successful kid entrepreneurs find their customers.

# CHAPTER 5

## NUTS & BOLTS OF LAUNCHING YOUR BUSINESS

# MARKETING MANIA

## The Essential Supplement to Door to Door Sales

Let's design a flyer for your business! We are going to be using Google Slides, a free, online program typically used for laying out presentations.

1. Navigate to **kidstartupbook.com/google-slides**

2. If you do not have a Google account, please register now with a parent's assistance.

3. Click the plus sign to create a new, blank presentation.

4. Select "Untitled Presentation" and change the name to, "Flyer."

5. Next, go to "File" -> "Page Setup." Then, select "Custom."

6. Type in the measurements shown here.

7. Select a theme from the right-hand side of the page.

8. Add the name of your company to the title. Add a subtitle that includes your name and phone number or email address.

9.  Navigate to "Insert" -> "Image..." and select an image from your computer.

10. Click on the image and drag a corner to change its size. Click and hold on the middle of the image and move it to wherever you would like.

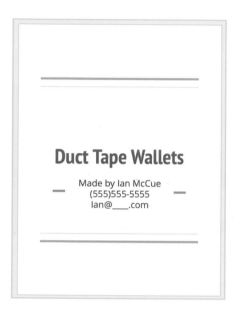

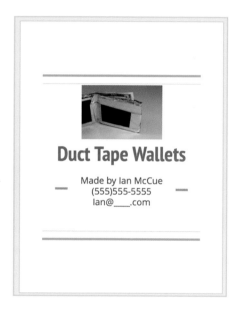

11. You have completed your flyer design! Click the printer icon and get ready to sell!

# SOCIAL MEDIA

## Stay Fresh in the Minds of Your Customers

A daily to weekly post helps your customers remember you. Let's get started using Pablo by Buffer, a website that helps you make beautiful posts. Try to use these in addition to actual photos of you and your business.

1.  Navigate to **kidstartupbook.com/pablo**

2.  Double-click to replace the text with a short message. We will use a snow shoveling company as our example.

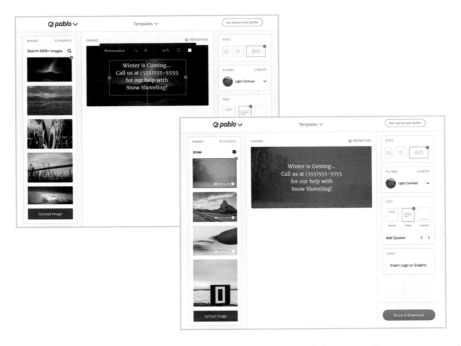

3. Click on the search box, type in a keyword for your business, and click enter. Click on an image to insert it.

4. Select Share & Download, and you're ready to go!

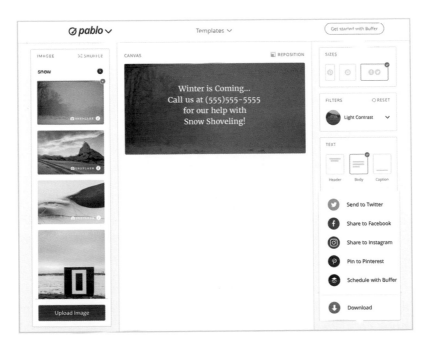

# BUILDING YOUR WEBSITE

## Your Online Business Portal

A great website sells your product 24/7. Invest some time upfront and benefit from increased sales for months to come!

1. Go to **kidstartupbook.com/weebly**

2. Click "Sign Up"

3. With a parent's permission, carefully complete the quick form to get started. Make sure that this is an email address that you can access!

4. Select a template of your choice. In web design, simple and easy is best.

5. Select to use a subdomain of Weebly.com. Enter the name of your business, replace spaces with dashes, and leave out special characters. For example, "Lucy's Lemonade" would become http://lucys-lemonade.weebly.com.

6. Highlight the title at the top of the page, and replace the text with the name of your business.

7. Navigate to the "Theme" tab at the top of the page. Click on "Change Fonts" then on "Site Title." Next, select the box next to color, and choose a color to represent your business.

8. Now that we've setup the essentials, watch Weebly's YouTube video on building out your website! You can find it at **kidstartup book.com/weebly-guide**

# SELLING ON EBAY

## A Massive Sales Channel for Your Products

Unfortunately, there are only so many friends and neighbors that you can sell your products to. Running out of customers? eBay has well over 100,000,000 people regularly making purchases.

1. Navigate to **kidstartupbook.com/ebay-sell**

2. Click "Create a Listing" and type in a title that describes your product. We will use scented soaps and title our product, "One Large Bar of Homemade Soap." Next, click "Sell it."

3. Select the condition as "New," and then click on "Continue."

4. Register with your parent's assistance.

5. Add pictures of your product, and select any accurate descriptions that appear.

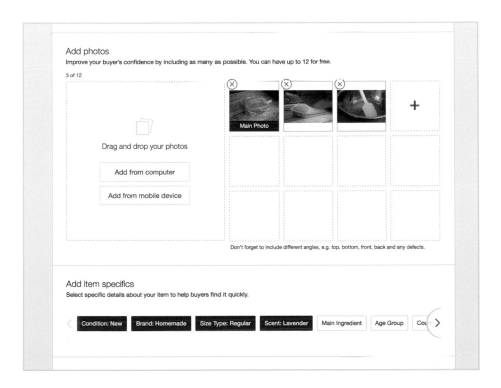

6. Enter a description, and feel free to mention that you are a small or kid business.

7. Choose to sell at a reasonable, fixed price. If you have a few of your product ready to sell, select "Sell more than one," and enter the quantity that you have.

8. Set shipping to be calculated by weight and size, and to be paid by the buyer.

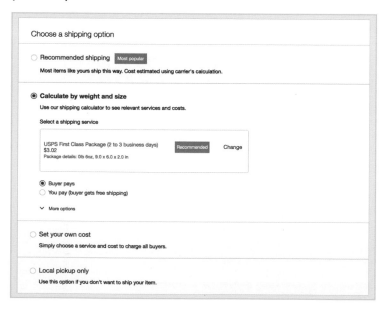

9. With your parent's approval, click "List it!" You're now ready to sell!

# LEGAL TIPS

Disclosure: This is not professional legal advice. We highly recommend consulting a small business attorney in your community.

* It is rare that a minor (someone under 18 years old) can start a business without an adult as a partner in it

* Parents will likely want to structure the company as a sole proprietorship (the cheapest method) and then pay their kid its profits as an allowance

* A sole proprietorship with a business name will typically be required to file for a DBA, which stands for "doing business as"

* Most businesses require a variety of business permits and/or licenses to operate legally

* Sellers of physical products may need to collect and pay a sales tax

* Profits will likely be subject to taxation

* Don't know where to start? Here are three great resources for small business owners:

    ◆ The Small Business Administration:
      **kidstartupbook.com/sba-start**

    ◆ LegalZoom or RocketLawyer:
      **kidstartupbook.com/legalzoom-start**
      **kidstartupbook.com/rocketlawyer-start**

    ◆ Local small business attorneys

CHAPTER **6**

## SUCCESSFUL KID ENTREPRENEUR
# INTERVIEWS

# BENJAMIN STERN

## Started Nohbo at age 14

## Creator of the First Eco-Friendly Shampoo Ball

Ben was inspired to make a difference when, at 14 years old, he viewed a video about the destructive impact of the plastic industry on our marine life. Ben envisioned a tab-like, single-use product that was water soluble for personal care products, such as shampoo, conditioner, body wash, and shaving cream. In early 2016, Ben appeared on ABC's "Shark Tank" to pitch his business, Nohbo, and ended up accepting a business offer from billionaire Mark Cuban.

**1. Did you have any business or work experience before you started your business?**
Nohbo wasn't my first company. I started a coffee subscription company, selling bags of coffee I bought at wholesale prices to neighbors, using the same model as typical school sales programs do. It was a nice business, but there was a limit to how big the business could get. That's when I realized I needed to create an invention.

**2. What inspired you to start your company?**
Escaping a job inspired me to create my own company. I saw my parents dislike their day jobs, and personally, I did not like working for others. I always had ideas, and ever since a young age, I've heard mentors, friends, teachers, etc. say that America was a place where opportunity exists for everyone. The word "everyone" does not have an age attached, so I saw

...y opportunity, had this amazing chance to grow it, and boom; my company was created.

### 3. What were the first steps that you took in starting your business?

The first step was to make sure others found my shampoo ball appealing. I did this by submitting the concept to companies like The Clorox Company and Hyatt Hotels. Following their positive reaction, I jumped on the idea and decided to turn this concept from nothing into a rolling stone. The next steps were finding legal counsel, saving up money, finding chemists, and just working out all the additional kinks in forming a startup.

### 4. What was your biggest challenge in starting a business?

I believe the biggest challenge in starting a business is, well, starting a business. Having an idea DOES NOT make you a business. Taking the first steps—like forming a legal company, building a website, and finding your base—makes you a business (...). In the beginning, you may have little to no emotional support, and through that process, you may be discouraged from continuing. It is commonly known that around 9 out of 10 startups fail. I don't believe that statistic; I think it's more like 9 out of 10 startups with some who really never started up, fail.

### 5. Do you have any advice for aspiring kid/teen entrepreneurs?

One of my favorite quotes is "He who hesitates is lost." Get up, create something cool, and never be discouraged by unknowledgeable people who have no idea what they're saying or doing! Only one person will make you who you want to be: you.

**6. Was there any one decision that was truly key to your company's success?**

Yes, building a strong team full of experts in their field has allowed the company to grow best. I was in a position where I could continue to hog some of the control, or give it to those who knew what they were doing better in their specific fields, so in order for me to avoid a certain mistake, they make decisions. Allowing others to make decisions has helped alleviate some of the stress from not only my shoulders, but everyone's.

**7. If you could go back in time and make one change to your business, what would it be?**

I believe the biggest change I would make is learning to prioritize better, so we would be in a position to invest more in research and development before getting ahead of ourselves. Growing slow is good, but too slow will allow your competitors to catch on and pass you.

**8. What do you want to be when you grow up?**

I consider myself grown up, and am doing what I want to be doing. Maybe I'll expand my field and expertise in the ever changing tech world, but I want to be running a business. I don't see myself retiring, even if I get to the point where I never need another dime for me or my family to live. This has turned into a game, and I just plain out love it.

**9. What have you learned through starting and running your business?**

I have learned a lot, but I think the number one lesson is don't lose your drive. For a while, business owners will be working for their company, nurturing it like a baby, to get it off the ground. It is hard, scratch that, this isn't hard. The beauty of what we do is it is something anyone can do; it can be very time consuming, tedious, tiresome, and at many times, just plain discouraging work, but I wouldn't describe it as hard. Anyways, you need something to be driving you to keep that excitement you first experienced when you thought of the idea and were encouraged to push it out to the public. Money is often an appealing end result, and I firmly believe it could be that driving force, but shouldn't be the only one. Think of what you are selling, and just enjoy the moments when a customer comes back with appreciation for what you've done. On a side note, never believe the myth that this will be fun all the time. It is an amazing experience nonetheless.

## 10. Why should fellow kids and teens start their own businesses?

Why not? You could succeed, and have experience, money, and even more opportunities, or you could fail, and still have experience and more opportunities than your peers. They say if one is under 35 years old, they can ALWAYS reaccumulate wealth to where it was. But for kids and teens, we have it even better. A house won't be foreclosed on us, a creditor won't be seeking a return, and we will always wake up and go to bed with food on our plates and a house over our head. Kids don't have to worry nearly as much about living expenses, which makes it a golden time to start.

# ANDREA CAO

- - - - - - - - - - - - - - - - - - - - - - - - - - - - - - - - -

## Started Q-Flex at age 13

## Creator of the Leading Self-Acupressure Device

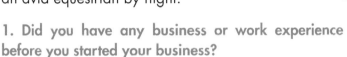

Andrea Cao is a 16-year-old CEO, entrepreneur, and horse trainer. She's been featured on Shark Tank, Beyond the Tank, Buzzfeed, Forbes, QVC, FOX, ABC, Inc., and Business Insider. She has become the youngest entrepreneur to host on QVC, and the youngest to have executive meetings at Walmart. Andrea is a hustling businesswoman by day and an avid equestrian by night.

**1. Did you have any business or work experience before you started your business?**
As a 13 year old, I couldn't really say that I had much work or business experience prior to starting Q-Flex. Looking back, however, I noticed that I really was born an entrepreneur. I had started all kinds of small businesses here and there, including selling live frogs and lizards to classmates, custom horse shampoo, and even my own line of trading cards. And that was just the beginning of it! While none of this generated much money, it fueled my spark and gave me priceless experiences that really set me up for starting my first "real" business.

**2. What inspired you to start your company?**
I was inspired to invent the Q-Flex when my mom would always come home with a sore back from work. I hated seeing her in pain and I couldn't really do much to help. I thought about how many other people must be suffering from the same issue, and as a joke, I

told myself, "Why don't I make something to fix that?" Well, if you knew 13-year-old Andrea, you would know that if she wants something, she works to make it happen. So what started out as a joke turned into a design on paper, which turned into a prototype, and eventually turned into an actual product!

**3. What were the first steps that you took in starting your business?**

After I had my first finished product in my hands, I did anything and everything I could to get the product out there. As a 13-year-old with essentially no formal marketing training or experience, it was quite the challenge. But, with high hopes I set out selling and pitching my product door to door, with each pitch getting stronger and me getting more confident! I became quite the saleswoman after those experiences, and those pitch skills landed me with deals in local health and fitness stores!

**4. What was your biggest challenge in starting a business?**

I would have to say that my biggest challenge at first was the age gap. I quickly shoved myself into a grown-up industry, and was often not taken seriously in the beginning. I had to say goodbye to the comforts of childhood and step into the real, intimidating world with big words and terms that I didn't quite understand. It pushed me to learn how to be comfortable when I'm the odd one out, which is something that I am super grateful for today.

**5. Do you have any advice for aspiring kid/teen entrepreneurs?**

You do you. Don't listen to the world telling you the big lie of "You can't." As an entrepreneur, you have to push yourself out of your comfort zone and learn to go against the grain. I am a firm believer that if you

want something bad enough, you'll find a way, and if not, you'll find excuses. You control how much effort you put forth, and it's going to reflect in your business and attitude, good or bad. When (not if) you fall, you get back up to see why you fell and how you can do better next time. Everything is a learning experience, so take advantage of it. And always remember that there are always going to be people seemingly more experienced, older, smarter, richer, etc., than you, but a river cuts through rock because of its persistence, not its power.

**6. Was there any one decision that was truly key to your company's success?**
Partnering with Mark Cuban and Barbara Corcoran on Shark Tank was huge. They took my business from a little girl going door to door and helped me turn it in to a million dollar, internationally recognized company. Both of them have taught me so many key lessons and values that I will use for the rest of my life.

**7. If you could go back in time and make one change to your business, what would it be?**
Honestly, I don't think I'd change a thing! I truly believe that this journey played out exactly how it was supposed to, and everything I've received (good or bad) has been a blessing that I am thankful for every day.

**8. What do you want to be when you grow up?**
As of now, I am a horse trainer and business owner, and I intend to keep it that way. I train wild mustangs, problem horses, and performance horses on my ranch as horses are my passion. I eventually want to start some equine companies because I know the market and the consumer very well (I am one haha!). I know that the moment I turn 18, I'm getting my real estate

license so I can invest in some rental homes and properties, because I love real estate.

**9. What have you learned through starting and running your business?**
Running my businesses has taught me too much to list in a couple of sentences, but to sum it up, I would have to say it has taught me a lot about life in general. I have developed so many key values and learnings which I know I will use my whole life. I have learned how to prioritize my time, manage my money, take calculated risks, and that's just the beginning of it. I have developed a strong work ethic, and an entrepreneurial mindset that sets me up for success. I know how to be independent and self-reliant to get things done myself.

**10. Why should fellow kids and teens start their own businesses?**
Starting your own business is the best decision you can make as a kid or teen. It'll teach you much more than you could ever learn in a classroom and make you a driven, strong, and awesome individual. Just like horses, a lot of young people need a job or a goal. If you find what you're passionate about and put your mind to it, you will go so far in life. Entrepreneurs are a different breed that live on different terms, and when we want something, we stop at nothing to get it. I can't think of anything more empowering than starting your own business and sticking with it. And who knows, you might even make some good money while you're at it.

# KATIE OSHINS

--------------------------------------------

## Started at age 11

## KObracelets, a Charitable Fashion Company

Katie spends her time learning, dancing, playing tennis, hanging out with her friends, and watching Netflix. Her favorite show is *Grey's Anatomy* which, along with her work for St. Jude, has inspired her to pursue medicine in the future.

**1. Did you have any business or work experience before you started your business?**
Yes, in 3rd grade I created a business also, in fact, for St. Jude's Children Hospital. I made duct tape bows and headbands and sold them. In the end I raised over $800 and donated all of the proceeds.

**2. What inspired you to start your company?**
Also in 3rd grade, I read a book written by Patricia Palacco, *The Lemonade Club*. It was about a whole class shaving their heads for a student who suffered with cancer. This really inspired me to help others in a way that the class did; however, I wasn't quite up to shaving my head at the time.

**3. What were the first steps that you took in starting your business?**
I asked myself three questions: 1. What am I good at? 2. What do I enjoy doing? 3. What is something a consumer would want? Once I settled on an idea, I made several prototypes and researched cost of materials. I also had to set up a time management plan so I could keep up with school and still have a social life.

**4. What was your biggest challenge in starting a business?**
My biggest struggle would probably be getting the word out about KObracelets. Once I had the product completed, how was I supposed to sell it? I went around the neighborhood selling them, utilized my family and friends, hosted jewelry parties to promote KObracelets, and marketed through social media. After the buzz got out, someone offered to collaborate with me and create a website.

**5. Do you have any advice for aspiring kid/teen entrepreneurs?**
I'd tell them when starting a business, do something that touches you and that you would enjoy. That way, you will have the motivation to keep going during hard times.

**6. Was there any one decision that was truly key to your company's success?**
Yes, creating a website that allowed me to reach out to people beyond my geographical location. Suddenly, I was being flooded with orders from various locations all around the world, such as New York, Florida, Australia, and Singapore.

**7. If you could go back in time and make one change to your business, what would it be?**
Honestly, though there were many challenges, I wouldn't change a thing at this point in the business. While there were tough decisions that had to be made, it was those decisions that taught me the most about entrepreneurship.

**8. What do you want to be when you grow up?**
I aspire to become a surgeon. I have always been interested in the medical field and would love to save the lives of more people one day.

**9. What have you learned through starting and running your business?**
I have learned that it takes a lot of perseverance, grit, and commitment in order to stick to the path you created for yourself. There will always be struggles and problems, but it's overcoming them that's key to success.

**10. Why should fellow kids and teens start their own businesses?**
Not only is it a great experience for the "real world," but in doing so, one feels accomplished and proud of who they have become. Some of the best feelings in the world are gratitude and pride. In addition, one is put in numerous situations in which they may have to step out of their comfort zones. This leads to tremendous growth.

# TAHOE MACK

Started at age 14

## CatchingYourDreamz, an Etsy art store

Tahoe has always loved personalization and self-expression, which is what inspired her to start her etsy shop. The art community motivated her to think outside the box and to make the world her own. She hopes to inspire young girls and boys to work towards being the best versions of themselves.

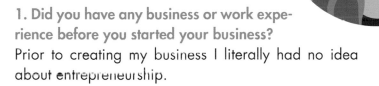

**1. Did you have any business or work experience before you started your business?**
Prior to creating my business I literally had no idea about entrepreneurship.

**2. What inspired you to start your company?**
Art has always inspired me to create different ways of expression, so I truely wanted to create something that individuals could use to show off their uniqueness!

**3. What were the first steps that you took in starting your business?**
First, I came up with an initial, broad plan. I wanted to make and sell dream catchers.

**4. What was your biggest challenge in starting a business?**
My biggest challenge was setting a correct price. Make sure you budget your time and pay yourself for hard work!

**5. Do you have any advice for aspiring kid/teen entrepreneurs?**
If you really want to accomplish something, big or small, don't limit yourself with negativity. If you create a clear path toward your dreams nothing can stand in your way!

**6. Was there any one decision that was truly key to your company's success?**
A turning point for my store was when I decided to branch off and create stickers. It was a huge step in a different direction but without it I may have not had my Etsy store today.

**7. If you could go back in time and make one change to your business, what would it be?**
I wish I had created more variations and gone even more in depth with my dreamcatchers.

**8. What do you want to be when you grow up?**
When I grow up, I want to own my own company that involves the art community.

**9. What have you learned through starting and running your business?**
I learned a lot about myself and what I am capable of. It gave me a lot of confidence in my ideas which pushes me forward every day.

**10. Why should fellow kids and teens start their own businesses?**
Starting your own business really puts you ahead of the game. It gives you not only the opportunity to experience the pleasure of self-reliance but also helps you understand how the economy works.

# TOMMY VANEK

## Started Selling Soap at Age 15

## Regularly Sells His Products in Bulk to Hotels

**1. Did you have any business or work experience before you started your business?**
I couldn't get a job before I was sixteen, but I took an entrepreneurship class in school that was really interesting and helped me make my decision to start a business.

**2. What inspired you to start your company?**
I wanted money for my first car. I chose soap because my family and I did a fun experiment making soap a few summers prior, so I chose to continue the experiment by making and selling soap.

**3. What were the first steps that you took in starting your business?**
I first had to run the numbers and figure out how much money it would take to start it up and how much I could sell it for to make a product. Then I had to get all of the permits and licenses required to start a business. Then I bought all of the materials and supplies needed to make the soap and I had to learn how to make it well. After all of that, I had to think of the names and designs of all of the soaps before I started production.

**4. What was your biggest challenge in starting a business?**
I think that one of the biggest challenges in starting up my business was the risk and hardship that came with it. Running a business can sometimes be extremely hard, and there is the possibility of losing the time and

money that you invest. I had to contact my suppliers and create a website and a million other things beside just making the soap that took up a lot of my time.

**5. Do you have any advice for aspiring kid/teen entrepreneurs?**
Don't be afraid to take risks. A lot of times, people won't do something because of the fear of failure. However, if something fails, then you can learn from it. It will often just be a bump in the road.

**6. Was there any one decision that was truly key to your company's success?**
I don't think that there was any one decision that made my company a success. It resulted from many small decisions, luck, and the support of my family.

**7. If you could go back in time and make one change to your business, what would it be?**
There isn't one big thing that I would change, but I would make a few small changes. I would be more careful when making the soap by staying on top of everything so that I don't ever have to rush at the last minute.

**8. What do you want to be when you grow up?**
To be honest, I have no idea what I want to be when I grow up, but probably something having to do with business or investing.

**9. What have you learned through starting and running your business?**
Running a business takes a lot of hard work and dedication, but it is definitely worth it. I recently bought my first car and I am loving every minute of it because I made the money through my working hard for my own business.

**10. Why should fellow kids and teens start their own businesses?**
It helped me learn a lot of responsibility and social skills. I have learned managerial skills, and, when I look at my business, I feel very proud of what I have created. It will also look great on resumes and college applications.

# EMILY MILLER

**Started at Age 15**

## Squishy USA, a squishy product creator

**1. Did you have any business or work experience before you started your business?**

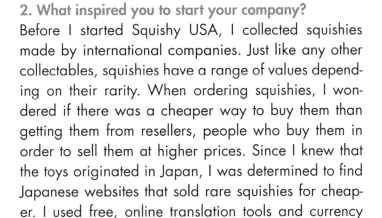

I did not, however I collected squishies for three years prior to creating Squishy USA. Because of this, I knew the brands and values of squishies via social media and interacting with people in the United States and other countries. When I started collecting squishies, they were much more popular internationally than they were domestically.

**2. What inspired you to start your company?**

Before I started Squishy USA, I collected squishies made by international companies. Just like any other collectables, squishies have a range of values depending on their rarity. When ordering squishies, I wondered if there was a cheaper way to buy them than getting them from resellers, people who buy them in order to sell them at higher prices. Since I knew that the toys originated in Japan, I was determined to find Japanese websites that sold rare squishies for cheaper. I used free, online translation tools and currency converters to learn about their products and pricing.

**3. What were the first steps that you took in starting your business?**

When I realized I could buy rare squishies for a fraction of the price in Japan, I decided to test the market and buy some squishies to resell on my Instagram account. At the time, I had around 1,000 followers from sharing photos of my collection of squishies. I used my social media following as an advantage to market the products. I sold my first squishies with a special promotion: I posted an image saying, "repost for $2 off" so that people who were thinking of purchasing would post the picture on their accounts and their followers would see it. That day, I earned around 300 followers, many of whom would be interested in purchasing my products. This success eventually earned me over 10,000 followers on my squishy Instagram account. I continued to buy and import collections from Japan.

### 4. What was your biggest challenge in starting a business?
The biggest challenges I faced were creating a market and bringing myself to take the risk. The goal in mind was to eventually design my own squishy and sell it on my account. Even though I knew I had the ability to design my own squishy, I had to get enough collectors interested because I'd be ordering and paying for hundreds of units. I would be investing a great sum of my earnings into something that I didn't know would succeed.

### 5. Do you have any advice for aspiring kid/teen entrepreneurs?
My advice would be to follow an idea you truly care about no matter how many people think it's weird or crazy. The crazy ideas are usually the ideas that are unique. Since squishies are foam collectables, I have spent four years of my life collecting foam. As a result, I used to get a ton of disagreement from my parents and some friends. As I started proving myself, my family and friends became very supportive of me.

### 6. Was there any one decision that was truly key to your company's success?
I feel like wholesaling was the key to my company's success. When I finally produced my unicorn squishy, I found that a lot of my audience was in countries such as Indonesia, Malaysia, the Philippines, and the United Kingdom. In order to get my product to my international followers, I did a good amount of wholesaling (selling in bulk) to local stores in those countries. International wholesaling helped me build a brand and sell my inventory more quickly.

**7. If you could go back in time and make one change to your business, what would it be?**
If I could change anything, I would've started a more aggressive social media platform because a larger account would have helped me in growing my business early on.

**8. What do you want to be when you grow up?**
I'm not too sure as of now, but I know that, whatever I do, I want it to be business oriented. Hopefully, I will continue to run my own business – I like the idea of being my own boss!

**9. What have you learned through starting and running your business?**
I've learned that building a business is complicated and takes patience to grow. Never before had I known all of the different components that go into starting a business. For example, I never knew of the marketing, designing, manufacturing, and shipping costs that go into selling squishies. In order for me to figure it out, I had to do research and accept lots of trial and error.

**10. Why should fellow kids and teens start their own businesses?**
Starting a business, especially if it involves something you truly care about, is a very rewarding process. For me, I always looked forward to going home and posting about new supplier packages and waiting for my own squishies to arrive. I also feel that starting a business has been a tremendous learning process that has helped me mature as a person.

# SUMMARY

-------------------------------------------

Kid entrepreneurs start with an idea for a product or service, but without business experience. It is often said that most businesses fail, when in fact most businesses *never even start*. Choose a simple product or service that you can make or provide, and start a business selling it. You do not need to know all of the details – you'll learn them on the way. Express your creativity in sales, and use internet platforms like Etsy to boost your sales!

## Key Takeaways

* You do not need to be an adult to start a business; in fact, it's even better to start as a kid! Start by selling a simple product or service.

* Kids don't have to worry nearly as much about living expenses as adults have do, which makes it a golden time to start a business.

* Starting your own business is the best decision you can make as a kid or teen. Becoming a kid entrepreneur will teach you much more than you could ever learn in a classroom and make you a driven, strong, and hard-working individual.

## Next Steps

Start TODAY! You do not need to be older, and you do not need a complicated business plan or a lot of money to start a business. All you need is an idea you love and the willingness to work hard at turning your dream into a reality.

CHAPTER **7**

## 10 BUSINESS PRINCIPLES
# ANY KID CAN FOLLOW

# BUSINESS PRINCIPLE #1: BUSINESS IDEAS ARE EASY

Now that you have learned how to discover your business idea and you've read about different business ideas that you can start, let's talk about how important ideas really are.

Good business ideas are everywhere. Having a good business idea is easy. Making a business out of that good idea is hard because it takes time and effort. Most kids don't have the time to pursue the great business ideas they have, and they aren't willing to put in the effort to make their idea a reality.

Many kids are fooled into thinking that what makes good businesses is the idea. The idea doesn't matter all that much. The execution is far more important.

A classic example of people putting too much value on the idea is the TV show Shark Tank. Shark Tank is so appealing to millions of people because people think to themselves, "Why didn't I think of that?" or "Wow, I could've thought of that simple idea."

Viewers are placing way too much importance on the idea of a particular product or service on the show. What most people don't realize is that the execution by the Shark Tank entrepreneurs is far more important.

There's often nothing all that special about the ideas that appear on Shark Tank. But it's the belief that ideas are so valuable that can often make the show addicting to watch. In reality, viewers should be admiring the hard work of the Shark Tank entrepreneurs instead.

You should always share your ideas with others too. For example, tell your idea to your family and friends to see what they think. Do not worry that others will steal your business idea. No one believes in your idea as much as you believe in your idea. Because most people will not believe in your idea, they will not put in the time and effort needed to pursue the idea.

There is no formula for coming up with good business ideas. Most of your best ideas will come to you when you're not actively trying to come up with brilliant ideas. You've probably had many great ideas yourself. However, you likely didn't pursue it because the execution of the idea was the hard part.

Later in this book, we'll discuss how to decide on the best idea, how to use the least resources and money to execute an idea, and ultimately how to best increase your chances to successfully start a new business. But for now, simply realize that good business ideas are easy to come up with...it's the execution that is the hard part.

## Practice

It's your turn to practice this Business Principle. In Chapter 4, you came up with a few business ideas. Now it's time to actually do these business ideas. Come up with an action plan below for each of your business ideas. Once you have your action plan written, decide which idea you want to actually turn into a real business that makes money!

# PRODUCT IDEA 1

### Idea

---

### Action Plan

How many hours per week will you need to work?

---

What materials will you need?

---

How much will it cost?

---

How much money will you make?

---

How will you sell your product or service (location, marketing, etc.)?

---

What steps will you take to make your idea a reality?

---

# PRODUCT IDEA 2

### Idea

- - - - - - - - - - - - - - - - - - - - - - - - - - - - - - - - - - - - - - - -

### Action Plan

How many hours per week will you need to work?

- - - - - - - - - - - - - - - - - - - - - - - - - - - - - - - - - - - - - - - -

What materials will you need?

- - - - - - - - - - - - - - - - - - - - - - - - - - - - - - - - - - - - - - - -

How much will it cost?

- - - - - - - - - - - - - - - - - - - - - - - - - - - - - - - - - - - - - - - -

How much money will you make?

- - - - - - - - - - - - - - - - - - - - - - - - - - - - - - - - - - - - - - - -

How will you sell your product or service (location, marketing, etc.)?

- - - - - - - - - - - - - - - - - - - - - - - - - - - - - - - - - - - - - - - -

- - - - - - - - - - - - - - - - - - - - - - - - - - - - - - - - - - - - - - - -

What steps will you take to make your idea a reality?

- - - - - - - - - - - - - - - - - - - - - - - - - - - - - - - - - - - - - - - -

- - - - - - - - - - - - - - - - - - - - - - - - - - - - - - - - - - - - - - - -

# SERVICE IDEA 1

## Idea

------------------------------------------------

### Action Plan

How many hours per week will you need to work?

------------------------------------------------

What materials will you need?

------------------------------------------------

How much will it cost?

------------------------------------------------

How much money will you make?

------------------------------------------------

How will you sell your product or service (location, marketing, etc.)?

------------------------------------------------

------------------------------------------------

What steps will you take to make your idea a reality?

------------------------------------------------

------------------------------------------------

# SERVICE IDEA 2

## Idea

---

## Action Plan

How many hours per week will you need to work?

---

What materials will you need?

---

How much will it cost?

---

How much money will you make?

---

How will you sell your product or service (location, marketing, etc.)?

---

---

What steps will you take to make your idea a reality?

---

---

# BUSINESS PRINCIPLE #2: DO WHAT YOU KNOW

Billionaire Warren Buffet has said that he is a successful investor because he invests only in businesses that he knows well. This could not be more true for entrepreneurs. The first rule of entrepreneurship is to Do What You Know.

At a speaking event with Timothy Ferris, a famous entrepreneur and the author of *The 4-Hour Workweek*, one of the attendees asked Ferris what kind of business the audience should think about starting. Ferris said, "Do something you have expertise [or skill] in." He said that he knew a lot about bodybuilding, so he started a sports nutrition company.

Many audience members were unhappy with his answer. They wanted Ferris to tell them exactly what kind of business they should start. He was the author of the 4-Hour Work Week after all. Shouldn't he have the secret to success? But in reality, this is the secret to success!

One of the biggest mistakes entrepreneurs make is attempting to start a business in something that they are not familiar with. If you have no knowledge of your new business' product or service, you are preventing yourself from being successful. But if you know a lot about your new business, you already have a huge advantage.

The second biggest mistake entrepreneurs make is not building massive value in the industry they plan to enter. There is no such thing as getting rich quick. Most people are not willing to put in the time and effort necessary to build massive value.

The 10,000 hour-rule from Malcolm Gladwell's famous book *Outliers* says that it takes 10,000 hours of practice in order to become a master at anything – sports, music, academics, etc. The same is true for business. Although it may not take 10,000 hours to build massive value, it will certainly take a lot of time and effort.

You might be thinking, "I don't know anything that well!" Don't worry, everyone thinks the same thing when they are first starting out. So let's do an exercise to help you think of some ideas. Answer the following three questions:

1. What topics would you consider yourself skillful at?

2. What is something you worked hard at in your life?

3. What are some of your greatest achievements in life?

How did that go? Hopefully you have generated some ideas. The best situation would be if there was one topic that showed up as an answer for all three questions. If that happened, you now know what industry you should start a business in.

If you weren't able to come up with some areas of skill that you have, then you need to become skillful in something. To become skillful, choose a topic that really interests you. Now, spend 100 hours learning everything you can about that topic. That's just step one of course. Then, spend 100 hours building a business for your future customers.

Notice that we don't have a really crazy formula for how to find your next business idea. As we learned before, good business ideas are every-where. But this principle took us one-step further and explained that good ideas are best turned into businesses by people who have great skill in those ideas. Turning the idea into a business is more important than the idea. Spend hundreds of hours building massive value in what you know to have the best chance of making your business idea a success.

## Practice

It's your turn to practice this Business Principle. Brainstorm ten things that you spend a lot of time doing already, that you love to do, or that you would love to learn how to do. Ready, go!

1 _____

2 _____

3 _____

4 _____

5 _____

6 _____

7 _____

8 _____

9 _____

10 _____

# BUSINESS PRINCIPLE #3: DON'T EXPECT TO WIN THE LOTTERY

On your path to making money, never expect to become a millionaire overnight.

The lottery is such an interesting thing. People are attracted by the idea of instantly winning money without working. People get even more interested in the lottery as the prize grows, even though their chances of winning go down.

Similar to the lotto, the bigger the market that you enter in business, the lower your chances of succeeding are because there is more competition. Unlike the lottery, instant millionaires are not born in business.

Today, the charm of overnight millionaires is more attractive than ever. Social media (Instagram, Snapchat, Facebook) provides instant gratification. You put a photo up, and it immediately gets likes. But if you put a product out, you will not immediately make money. On social media, you may see a video go viral that causes an unknown person to become an instant success. But you should treat these viral successes like the lottery — an unlikely possibility.

You can surely be a success. But you will surely not be an overnight success. Patience is a virtue. You must be willing to put in the effort necessary to grind it out through the tough times, especially in the beginning — when most kids would quit. You likely have a winning idea, you just don't know it yet. Stop wishing to win the lotto with your idea and start putting in more effort than anyone else around you — it will pay off.

## Practice

It's your turn to practice this Business Principle. Let's say that you run a dog walking business (see Chapter 5 for more information on how to start this business). Each dog that you walk makes you $10.

Don't expect to win the lottery. It is unlikely that you will walk one hundred dogs in the first month. Instead, you might walk just one. But if you continue to put in effort, you might double the number of dogs you walk each month because more people will want you to walk their dogs once they hear about how good you are. Let's see what happens to your business if you double the number of dogs you walk each month:

| Month 1 | Walk **1 Dog** | $ 10 profit |
| Month 2 | Walk **2 Dogs** | $ _ _ _ Profit |
| Month 3 | Walk **4 Dogs** | $ _ _ _ Profit |
| Month 4 | Walk **8 Dogs** | $ _ _ _ Profit |
| Month 5 | Walk **16 Dogs** | $ _ _ _ Profit |
| Month 6 | Walk **32 Dogs** | $ _ _ _ Profit |
| Month 7 | Walk **64 Dogs** | $ _ _ _ Profit |
| Month 8 | Walk **128 Dogs** | $ _ _ _ Profit |

If you did your math correctly, you could make over $1000 per month with this business by month 8!

Most kids would want to make $1000 right away when starting a business. Once they don't make a large amount of money very quickly, they stop trying altogether.

But notice what happens if you are patient. By month 8, you are making over $1000 per month with your business! Of course, you will learn that businesses can't keep doubling their sales every month forever, but it is certainly possible in the first few months.

Your business can also be limited by the amount of time you have. For example, it is unlikely that you have time to walk 128 dogs yourself. At that point, you might want to hire other kids to help you walk dogs and pay them some of your profits. You are officially a business owner with employees!

# BUSINESS PRINCIPLE #4: SAVE MONEY TO MAKE MONEY

Benjamin Franklin said, "A penny saved is a penny earned." This is certainly true for your personal savings. Figure out a way to save $5 to $10 a week. By the end of the month, deposit your extra cash into a bank account. It may not seem like a lot at first, but over time, your bank account will grow a lot. This is not really due to the little bit of money that you are saving, but more due to the idea of savings eventually becoming a good part of your life.

Mark Cuban certainly tried to save money growing up. Mark chose to go to Indiana University because it had the least expensive tuition. He used to sleep on the floor in college and have a closet as his room. Mark's simple idea of saving money has led to much of his success.

Saving money is especially important when it comes to business. For example, don't start your business on a loan. A loan is money that a bank gives you, but that you must pay it back, plus extra, in a few years. Starting something as high- risk as a new business with something as high-risk as a loan is probably not a good idea, especially for kids. Instead, find different ways to fund your idea. Most Internet businesses can be started for almost no money because of the many free and cheap web tools available. If your business does require a lot of money to start, try saving enough money by working a job first, start a crowdfunding campaign, or try starting a different business that does not require as much money to start.

When you are running your business, try to find lower cost ways to get your materials. For example, if you need duct tape to build duct tape wallets that you are selling, then see if you can buy the duct tape in bulk or online for cheaper than buying one roll at the store (see Chapter 5 for more information on how to start this business). The more money you can save, the more money you will make. But don't be too cheap in making your products such that the quality is bad.

## Practice

It's your turn to practice this Business Principle. Let's say that you run shoelace business (see Chapter 5 for more information on how to start this business). Below are different white shoelaces that you can buy from different stores. Which store should you buy shoelaces from in order to get the lowest cost per shoelace?

| STORE | SHOELACE SET | PRICE |
|-------|--------------|-------|
| Wal-Mart | 1 Shoelace | $1.00 |
| Target | 2 Shoelaces | $2.50 |
| **Costco** | **10 Shoelaces** | **$8.00** |

You should purchase the shoelaces from Costco! Why? Because each shoelace would only cost you **$0.80 ($8.00 / 10 Shoelaces = $0.80)**.

This is cheaper than buying shoelaces from either Wal-Mart ($1 per shoelace) or Target ($1.25 shoelace). By saving money in your business, you are actually making money for yourself because you get to keep the extra savings!

# BUSINESS PRINCIPLE #5: BE A BIG FISH IN A SMALL POND

One good way to increase your chances of business success is to be a big fish in a small pond. In other words, it's better to enter a small market with less competition than it is to enter a large market with a lot of competition.

This strategy mainly refers to physical places. You have a higher chance of success in a small town than a large city. For kid entrepreneurs, consider setting up shop in a small neighborhood, not a large one. Your business will likely do much better in an environment where you are not surrounded by competition. A bigger market does not always equal greater sales.

For example, let's say that you are considering opening a lemonade stand (see Chapter 5 for more information on how to start this business). Instead of opening a lemonade stand nearby another lemonade stand that another kid has started, you should consider opening your lemonade stand away from similar competition. Of course, you still want to be in a region that has a lot of people. But it's much better to be the only lemonade stand in a place that has 100 visitors a day than it is to be one of ten lemonade stands in a place that has 500 visitors a day.

This strategy can also apply to choosing the business you are going to start. You have a higher chance of success starting a business that only a few people in your area are already doing rather than starting a business that many people in your area are already doing. Do a quick Google search to see how many businesses related to the one that you are starting already exist, and pay extra attention to the ones that are in your area.

Be a big fish in a small pond to increase your chances of business success.

## Practice

It's your turn to practice this Business Principle. Let's say that you run a car wash business (see Chapter 5 for more information on how to start this business). Below is a map of all of the car wash locations in your area. Which point on the map would be best to open your car wash location?

A. Location 1     B. Location 2     **C. Location 3**     D. Location 4     E. Location 5

The best spot on the map to open your car wash would be at **Location 3**. Because Location 3 is the furthest from the other car washes on the map, it is likely that you will face less competition in this area. Opening a car wash at Location 1, Location 2, Location 4, or Location 5 would result in tough competition from other car washes. Try to stay away from a crowded market. Be a big fish in a small pond!

# BUSINESS PRINCIPLE #6: MAKE MONEY IN YOUR SLEEP

Trading your time for money will never lead to significant wealth. You only have 8,760 hours in a year, and much of that is spent sleeping. You must set up businesses that continue to make money even when you sleep.

Passive income (making money while you are not working) is the key to real wealth. More than half of the world's billionaires started their own businesses. Starting a business is probably the most common way to make passive income.

Of course, it's not easy to start a successful business — half of small businesses fail within the first five years. That's why this entire book is dedicated to help you learning how to start a business at a young age. We hope that eventually, you will be able to start a business that makes you money while you sleep. But first, let's understand why passive income is so important.

Doctors, lawyers, engineers, and other professionals are essentially highly skilled laborers, trading time for money. But there is a ceiling on the money they can earn. That ceiling is the number of hours that they can work.

This is not to say that you should not go to school to have a professional career and start a business instead. The two do not have to be completely separate. Highly skilled professionals are often the best people to start businesses. To start a successful business, you must first create value. And specific expertise in a particular area can have a lot of value. But most professionals sell value according to how much time they can work. Instead, professionals should sell value by starting a business that is not limited by their time.

The good news about generating a passive income stream is that it is easier than ever because of the Internet. Fifty years ago, creating a passive income stream was difficult. To build a business, you'd have to invest in a building and were limited by location and hours. Now, the

Internet makes it almost free to open a store that's open 24 hours a day to billions of customers worldwide. The Internet has made it easier than ever to make money in your sleep.

## Practice

It's your turn to practice this Business Principle. Even though your first business might not sell products or services online, one day you will likely want to start a business that sells items on the Internet. This will open up the door for people around the world to be able to buy your products and services. A few places that you might want to consider selling your items first would be eBay or Etsy since these will make a webpage for you so that people can purchase your items.

In the space below, brainstorm some ideas for products or services that you would like to sell online. Using the Internet to sell your items online will be the easiest way for you to start making money in your sleep. It may be 2:00AM in the morning, but the duct tape wallet that you are selling on Etsy might still sell online – that is the beauty of the Internet!

### PRODUCTS & SERVICES TO SELL ONLINE

1
2
3
4
5
6
7
8
9
10

# BUSINESS PRINCIPLE #7: JUST START

Entrepreneurs have too much fear about having the perfect start for their product or service. Stop being so exact. Just start your business and change it as you go.

Too many people worry way too much about customer feedback, researching the market, and their competition before they have even released a product or service. It gets so bad that many people delay starting their business or don't start at all.

*The Lean Start-Up* by Eric Ries is the most famous book on entrepreneurship. It is all that is talked about in entrepreneurship classes and conferences. But the problem with the lean start-up method is that it is easy to get bogged down in all of the customer feedback. You make the mistake of trying to be everything to everyone. But you can't, and won't, make everyone happy.

Instead, try the Steve Jobs approach: people don't know what they want. If Steve Jobs, the founder of Apple, had asked for customer feedback about old flip phones back in 2003, do you think any customer would have said they wanted a mobile device that you can interact with completely with touch? Probably not, and the iPhone would have never been created. Henry Ford, the founder of the Ford car company, is also famous for saying, "If I had asked people what they wanted, they would have said faster horses." And the Ford car would have never been created back in 1903.

So how can you reduce the risk of creating something that people will not use? Create a product or service that you yourself would use and pay for. If you are the customer for your product or service, you have all the feedback you need. Start something that you yourself would love, rather than trying to build something that some person you know nothing about would hopefully love because you have a guess that they will love it.

Finally, ignore the competition. Many entrepreneurs do way too much research into the competition. Once you understand some basic points about your competition such as service offerings and price points, move on. Focus on building your own business, not following someone else's.

## Practice

It's your turn to practice this Business Principle. Take one of the ideas for an online business that you wrote down in the practice section of the last Business Principle (Make Money In Your Sleep) and build a website selling the product or service! You don't have to actually build the product or service you are thinking of starting just yet. Instead, you just need the idea of a business.

Whatever product or service you are thinking of creating, start a website describing what it is and set a launch date three months from now. Setup a payment system for people to preorder your product or service (have your parents help you with this part since you may need a PayPal account or other payment processor). If you get people ordering your product or service, make sure you create your product or service. If you don't get anyone ordering your product or service, you don't have to build your product or service at all.

# BUSINESS PRINCIPLE #8: BE OBSESSED

A successful kid entrepreneur needs to be obsessed with his or her goals. In order to succeed, you must think about your business all day everyday.

Obsession is different from passion. Obsession is thinking about something all the time whereas passion is excitement. You don't need to be passionate about what you are creating, but you do need to be obsessed with creating it.

Developing an obsession is important because as an entrepreneur you have to be the hardest working person in the room. Mark Cuban often says, "Work like there's someone working 24 hours a day to take it all away from you." His Shark Tank co-star Lori Greiner says, "Entrepreneurs are willing to work 80 hours a week to avoid working 40 hours a week." In order to work so hard, you will need to be obsessed with what you are creating. If you are not, you will burnout.

Business school can sometimes make people hesitant to become entrepreneurs. The problem with business school is that it tries to turn entrepreneurship into a science. But entrepreneurship is not a science, it is an art. If you listen to an economics professor, you would think there would be no way to start a successful business because you would get crushed by the competition and there are no profits in the long-run.

But sometimes it's better to ignore logic and reason, and follow your obsession. The successful entrepreneur has to be a naive, wide-eyed, hopeful kid who believes he or she can do what no one else can — succeed against all odds.

## Practice

It's your turn to practice this Business Principle.

To develop an obsession, we do not suggest listing your passions. As stated previously, there is a small difference between an obsession and a passion. Of course, it is possible to be both passionate and obsessed with the same thing. Instead, decide what you can do better than anyone else on this planet. If you really believe you have the knowledge, tools, and expertise to do something ten times better than the next guy, then you will likely develop an obsession to prove that.

Developing an obsession might make others think you are crazy. You'll have to be careful between being crazy and being a genius. When you are first starting your business, everyone will think that you are crazy. But when you succeed, everyone will think you are a genius.

List a few things you are obsessed with below.

1 _____

2 _____

3 _____

4 _____

5 _____

6 _____

7 _____

8 _____

9 _____

10 _____

# BUSINESS PRINCIPLE #9:
# GIVE SOMETHING TO GET SOMETHING

Most people will not buy your product or service immediately because it is not the right time for them to purchase it. Do not lose these customer leads that may buy from you later. In order to do this, give them something for free now so that you are at the top of their mind when they are ready to make a purchase later.

If you have an in-person business that sells products, then you may want to give a sample of your products away for free (if it is not too expensive for you to give a sample away).

If you have an in-person business that sells services, then you may want to offer your first service for free (if it is not too expensive for you to offer one free service).

If you have an Internet business, then Internet marketing has a golden rule: "content is king." However, this is incorrect. It should be "free content is king." In other words, you must be willing to give away some portion of your product or service, or at least some knowledge about it, in order to generate interest from potential customers.

The best way to do marketing on the Internet is not to do any marketing. In other words, don't yell at the top of your lungs.

"My product is the best in the world! You should try it because of this and that!"

People don't respond to direct marketing — it's too loud and in-your-face. Instead, you should try something like the following:

"Download My Top 10 Tips On How To…"

People will respond much better because they love free.

But there is no such thing as a free lunch. If you are giving away something highly valuable to potential customers, they should be willing to give you something: an e-mail address. You want to collect the e-mail addresses of potential customers because it allows you to connect with them later with more free offers, tips, and eventually an offer to purchase your product or service.

## Practice

It's your turn to practice this Business Principle.

Create a short 10-page eBook with 10 tips related to a topic that you are an expert in. Now, release one of these tips each week on your website's blog. At the end of each blog post, write that people can download your free eBook by simply entering their e-mail into a form. You can use web tools such as LeadPages and MailChimp to capture e-mails. Make sure to get their permission to e-mail them later about more free tips and future offers.

If you don't want to create an eBook, you can also have a contest to give away free products or services from your business, and have people enter the contest by entering their e-mail address so that you have their contact information.

In any case, it doesn't really matter what content you give out (an eBook, a product sample, etc.). Just make sure that it's inexpensive for you to give out for free and that it is very valuable for your potential customers. By building your e-mail list of potential leads, you will create a profitable business in no time.

# BUSINESS PRINCIPLE #10: START A SERVICE-BASED BUSINESS

We've talked a lot in this book about both products and services. While we suggest launching your first company as a product-business, eventually you may want to consider launching a service-business.

Starting a service-based business usually costs less money and has a higher probability of success than a product-based business for the kid entrepreneur.

When you think of a creative entrepreneur, you typically think of an inventor who experiments with materials to create a new product. But we want you to reimagine your image of a creative entrepreneur as someone who produces value by providing a service. In fact, with every new season of Shark Tank, more and more service-based companies and apps are appearing on the show.

Technology companies used to sell software as a product. They now sell it as a service. In recent years, the trend in the software industry has been to sell SAS, or Software As a Service. This way, software is paid for every month rather than once. This not only increases the profits of software companies, but it also helps to reduce the copying of their services by hackers (also known as piracy).

But whether you are creating an Internet service or an in-person service (or both), your strategy when creating a service-based business should remain the same: Your service needs to be effective and deliver results.

## Practice

When thinking about starting a service-based company, you need to think about user experience. A user experience is the experience that a customer has when using your product or service.

For example, when you go to order a hamburger at McDonald's, the user experience may be that you place your order at the first window using a telecom and then pay for and pickup your order at the second window. But let's be creative! How could you improve the user experience of the McDonald's drive- thru? Perhaps you could have a touchscreen computer that lets customers select what they want off the menu so that they don't need to talk to anyone through a hard-to-hear telecom. This is just one idea on how you could improve the user experience of the McDonald's drive-thru.

When you create a service-based company, you need to think about how to make the customer user experience as amazing as possible. Always think about how to improve the user experience in your service-based company to make it easier, more fun, or better for customers.

List the user experience of various products or services that you currently use. Under each one, list how the user experience could be improved in order to make the product or service better for the customer.

## Service 1

User Experience:

- - - - - - - - - - - - - - - - - - - - - - - - - - - - - - - - - - - - - - - - - - - - - - - - - -

How To Improve the User Experience:

- - - - - - - - - - - - - - - - - - - - - - - - - - - - - - - - - - - - - - - - - - - - - - - - - -

## Service 2

User Experience:

- - - - - - - - - - - - - - - - - - - - - - - - - - - - - - - - - - - - - - - - - - - - - - - - - -

How To Improve the User Experience:

- - - - - - - - - - - - - - - - - - - - - - - - - - - - - - - - - - - - - - - - - - - - - - - - - -

## Product 1

User Experience:

- - - - - - - - - - - - - - - - - - - - - - - - - - - - - - - - - - - - - - - - - - - - - - - - - -

How To Improve the User Experience:

- - - - - - - - - - - - - - - - - - - - - - - - - - - - - - - - - - - - - - - - - - - - - - - - - -

## Product 2

User Experience:

- - - - - - - - - - - - - - - - - - - - - - - - - - - - - - - - - - - - - - - - - - - - - - - - - -

How To Improve the User Experience:

- - - - - - - - - - - - - - - - - - - - - - - - - - - - - - - - - - - - - - - - - - - - - - - - - -

# SUMMARY

Many of these business principles go against common thoughts. People often discuss business ideas, but they ignore execution — the actions that can turn almost any idea into a successful business. Long business plans are not necessary. Just start! Do not expect to win the lottery, but know that your hard work will pay off.

## Key Takeaways

* Great execution, not an idea, is the key to success in business.

* Do what you know, and be obsessed with it.

* Start your business — most businesses fail because they never start!

## Next Steps:

Start a business today doing something that you know, especially a service. Obsess over your business, and focus on execution, not ideas. Skip the lengthy business plan — just start!

# CHAPTER 8

# EXTRA CONTENT

# AFFILIATE MARKETING

People tell their family and friends about their favorite products all the time, and this free marketing is *very* valuable to businesses. However, not everyone can be a customer! If you sell dog walking, then a friend without dogs cannot purchase your service. This friend is not likely to tell their friends and family about your products or services because they have not purchased your offerings themselves.

You may want to motivate people who are not your customers to recommend your offerings by paying them for every new customer that they send to you. People who recommend your business to customers in exchange for money are called affiliates.

Not every business uses affiliates to market its products and services. If you sell inexpensive products like water bottles or lemonade, then you should probably not have affiliates. If you sell more expensive services, such as car washes or dog walking, then affiliates can be amazing for your business.

## Practice

Start selling your products with affiliates today by offering your friends a couple of dollars for every new customer that they send to you. Pay them just enough to motivate them while keeping most of the profit for yourself!

# GLOSSARY

- ★ Brand: a name that a business gives it products; small businesses often use the same name for their brand and their business

- ★ Business: a person or a group of people that sell a specific set of products or services, often of its own brand

- ★ Buy: to give a person or company money in exchange for a good or service

- ★ Company: another word for business

- ★ Cost: the amount of money that you must spend to make your product or to provide your service; includes the cost of materials such as duct tape

- ★ Customer: someone who buys your product or service

- ★ Entrepreneur: a person who starts a business to help people and make money

- ★ Foot Traffic: the number of people who walk by your storefront (or stand) on any given day

- ★ Founder: another word for entrepreneur

- ★ Free Trial: a free offering of your product or service to new potential customers with the hope that they will buy from you in the future

- ★ Good: another word for product

- ★ Ideal Price: the price at which you will make the most profit from your product or service

- ★ Invention: a new device or process created by experimentation or experience

- ★ Marketing: the ways that you find people to buy products and services from your business

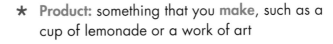

* **Product:** something that you **make**, such as a cup of lemonade or a work of art

* **Price:** the amount of money that you sell your product or service for

* **Profit:** the amount of money left over when you subtract your cost from your price

* **Purchase:** another word for buy

* **Referral Marketing:** a type of marketing that uses your customers to spread the word about your product or service; they buy your product or service, and they tell their friends about it

* **Revenue:** the amount of money that you make from selling your product or service before subtracting costs

* **Sell:** to exchange your product or service for money

* **Service:** something that you **do** for someone, such as walking their dog or shoveling their snow

* **Startup:** a new business that has recently begun operations

* **Talent:** a natural ability or skill

* **Wholesale:** The sale of products in large quantities, often at discounted prices

# RESOURCES

## WEBSITE BUILDERS:
## Your Presence in the Digital World

* Squarespace – simple, modern templates that are great
  for service-based businesses
  **kidstartupbook.com/squarespace-websites**

* Shopify – excellent online storefronts for product-based companies
  **kidstartupbook.com/shopify**

* Wix and Weebly – free websites with limited features,
  ideal for getting started without collecting payments online
  **kidstartupbook.com/wix or /weebly**

* Square – this payment processor enables
  you to build an online store at no cost
  **kidstartupbook.com/square-websites**

## LOGO & GRAPHICS SOURCES:
## Great Logos and Images for Growing Companies

* 99designs – this crowdsourced platform enables
  you to setup a logo-design competition
  **kidstartupbook.com/99designs**

* Squarespace – offers a simple logo builder with countless graphics
  **kidstartupbook.com/squarespace-logo**

* UpWork – hire professional designers from around the globe
  **kidstartupbook.com/upwork**

* StockSnap – free stock images for use on your website and flyers
  **kidstartupbook.com/stocksnap**

## PAYMENT PROCESSORS:
## Accept Non-Cash Payment for Your Goods or Services

* Square – swipe credit and debit cards in
  person on your smartphone
  **kidstartupbook.com/square-payments**

* Stripe – built into Squarespace and many other website builders, Stripe enables an easy online checkout **kidstartupbook.com/stripe**

* PayPal – this classic digital wallet enables you to accept payments from credit cards and other PayPal accounts with minimal effort **kidstartupbook.com/paypal**

## APP BUILDERS:
### The Best Mobile Experience You Can Offer

* Shoutem – easily build loyalty apps to reward your customers, inform them of events, and more **kidstartupbook.com/shoutem**

* GameSalad – interested in making your own mobile games? GameSalad enables the fastest route to a live app on iOS and Android devices **kidstartupbook.com/gamesalad**

## GRAPHICS GALAXY:
### Design Your Own Logo, Ads, and More!

* Adobe Illustrator – the industry standard of graphic design software **kidstartupbook.com/adobe-illustrator**

* Sketch – a modern graphics design tool for all purposes **kidstartupbook.com/sketch**

* Microsoft PowerPoint – a presentation builder capable of generating simple graphics and layouts **kidstartupbook.com/powerpoint**

## PRO PRINTERS:
### Postcards, Brochures, and More!

* Primo Print – ready to go big? order high quality printed materials of all sorts **kidstartupbook.com/primoprint**

* Vistaprint – the go-to budget business card printer
**kidstartupbook.com/vistaprint**

* Moo –high quality business cards sure to make an impression
**kidstartupbook.com/moo**

## SAVE ON SUPPLIES:
### The Best Online Stores for Your Business Needs

* Jet – the budget competitor to Amazon.com
**kidstartupbook.com/jet**

* Amazon – if you can't find something on Jet
**kidstartupbook.com/amazon**

* Michaels – artistic supplies perfect for your craft products
**kidstartupbook.com/michaels**

## OTHER RESOURCES

* Udemy – a huge online course library with all sorts
of courses that could help you in running your business
**kidstartupbook.com/udemy**

* Rocket Lawyer – a one-stop shop for almost
every common legal document
**kidstartupbook.com/rocket-lawyer**

* SBA – the government's guidance department for small businesses
**kidstartupbook.com/sba**

* Wave – free accounting software to help you
manage your revenue and costs
**kidstartupbook.com/wave**

# ACKNOWLEDGMENTS

We would like to thank Lorena Molinari for her excellent illustrations throughout the book, and Danielle Lincoln Hanna and Lia Ottaviano for their excellent work as editors.

We would also like to express appreciation to Shayna Indyg for her photos and guide in "Scented Soaps," Nick Tehle, Iris Weisman, and Iris' son Brad for contributions to "Car Wash Craze," and Atri for his contribution to "Water Bottles."

We especially appreciate Camille McCue, Blythe Cherney, Kendal Martin, Robin Oshins, Rachel Ziter, and the students of the Adelson Educational Campus for their input on an advance copy of the book, as well as Victoria Lopez, Skarlett Severson, Dylan Kai Hasimoto, Alexander Matthew Caday, Sahil Bhatnagar, Devika Bhatnagar, Ailla Nancarrow, Isabel Dorado-gentry, Zara Pehlivani, Farah Purewal, Kaiya Elle Kakita, and Skylar Segovia for taking the time to attend and provide feedback in a focus group setting.